BACK FROM NEAR EXTINCTION
CALIFORNIA
CONDOR

by Amanda Lanser

Content Consultant
Janet A. Hamber
Condor Conservationist
Santa Barbara Museum of Natural History

Core Library

An Imprint of Abdo Publishing
abdopublishing.com

abdopublishing.com

Published by Abdo Publishing, a division of ABDO, PO Box 398166, Minneapolis, Minnesota 55439. Copyright © 2017 by Abdo Consulting Group, Inc. International copyrights reserved in all countries. No part of this book may be reproduced in any form without written permission from the publisher. Core Library™ is a trademark and logo of Abdo Publishing.

Printed in the United States of America, North Mankato, Minnesota
092016
012017

Cover Photo: Shutterstock Images
Interior Photos: Shutterstock Images, 1, 16 (middle), 16 (bottom); Kent Weakley/Shutterstock Images, 4; Red Line Editorial, 7; Kim Worrell/Shutterstock Images, 10, 43; JPL Designs/Shutterstock Images, 12; Joseph Brandt/US Fish and Wildlife Service, 14; George Peters/iStockphoto, 16 (top); Andrew Zarivny/Shutterstock Images, 18; California Department of Fish and Wildlife, 21; Sascha Corti/Shutterstock Images, 23; Handout/Bellingham Herald/MCT/Newscom, 24; Jon Myatt/US Fish and Wildlife Service, 28; Charlie Neuman/U-T San Diego/ZumaPress/Newscom, 31, 45; ZSSD/ Minden Pictures/Newscom, 33; US Fish and Wildlife Service, 35; Ben Margot/AP Images, 36; Nick Ut/AP Images, 39

Editor: Marie Pearson
Series Designer: Jake Nordby

Publisher's Cataloging-in-Publication Data

Names: Lanser, Amanda, author.
Title: California condor / by Amanda Lanser.
Description: Minneapolis, MN : Abdo Publishing, 2017. | Series: Back from near
    extinction | Includes bibliographical references and index.
Identifiers: LCCN 2016945428 | ISBN 9781680784657 (lib. bdg.) |
    ISBN 9781680798500 (ebook)
Subjects: LCSH: California condor--Juvenile literature.
Classification: DDC 598.9--dc23
LC record available at http://lccn.loc.gov/2016945428

CONTENTS

SOARING THE SOUTHWEST AGAIN

Number 187 leaps from the Grand Canyon's towering cliffs and into the sky. Once in flight, the male California condor soars thousands of feet above the canyon's floor. His 9-foot (3-m) wingspan cuts a silhouette against the blue sky. He might soar hundreds of miles looking for carrion to eat. Riding the rising air currents, 187 rarely has to flap his wings to stay aloft.

In 2014 there were 73 wild condors in northern Arizona and southern Utah. Several of these lived in the Grand Canyon.

In April 2016, 187 nested on the Battleship rock formation with his mate, 280. They had used the nesting site before. Scientists monitor the pair's behavior. The birds are two of just 78 California condors in Arizona. There are only 230 wild condors today. The hopes of conservationists rest on the breeding success of these wild birds. One day, people hope to see thousands of condors soaring the skies of the US Southwest.

Soaring Toward Extinction

In 1982 that day seemed unreachable. Only 22 wild California condors existed in the world. The birds were at risk of extinction.

Condors in Native American Traditions

California condors have an honored place in many Californian Native American traditions. Ancient peoples made condor bone whistles. These artifacts are up to 10,000 years old. Later California tribes used condor skin and feathers in their mourning ceremonies. The Chumash fletched arrows with feathers. They threaded feathers into jewelry and clothing.

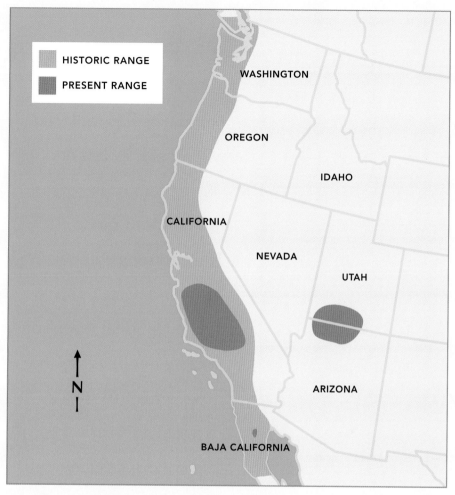

California Condor Range Today

Study this map of the condor's range today. What do you notice about the areas it lives in? What does it tell you about the condor's status today compared to its status in the past?

Condors are scavengers. They eat the remains of dead animals. Hunters and ranchers shot some of these animals. The lead from bullets poisoned condors. Many died.

Chick Ackaw

On April 1, 2016, the San Diego Zoo Safari Park welcomed its newest condor. Ackaw weighed just 6 ounces (170 g) when he pecked through his shell. He did not hatch with his parents' sleek, black feathers. Instead, Ackaw was covered in fluffy, white down. He spent most of his first months sleeping and growing. Visitors and bird enthusiasts watched Ackaw's progress on the zoo's 24-hour Condor Cam.

Meanwhile, humans moved in on condor habitat. Towns replaced wilderness. Roads and power lines crisscrossed the condor's range. The condor's numbers dwindled. Groups such as the National Audubon Society (NAS) asked the government to step in to protect the condors. The condor became one of the first species the Endangered Species Act protected in 1973. In 1987 the last wild condor was brought to the San Diego Zoo Safari Park. Conservationists wanted to protect all remaining condors. The birds were now extinct in the wild.

Conservationists Take Action

Since the early 1900s, conservationists have worked to bring the condor back from the brink. Today federal and state agencies partner with zoos and nonprofit organizations in conservation efforts. Some laws protect condors from being hunted. Others ban lead ammunition in condor habitats.

Zoos and the Peregrine Fund raise condors in captivity. Some birds continue to live and breed in captivity. Others are released into the wild. Thanks to these breeding programs, condors again live in the wild.

FURTHER EVIDENCE

Chapter One introduced you to the threats California condors face. What was one of the chapter's main points? What key evidence supports this point? Visit the website about lead poisoning below. Does it present more evidence to support the main point?

Lead Bullet Risks for Wildlife & Humans

mycorelibrary.com/california-condor

CHAPTER TWO

ABOUT THE CONDOR

California condors are members of the Cathartidae family. This family includes vultures and condors of the Western Hemisphere. The California condor's scientific name is *Gymnogyps californianus*. *Gymnogyps* means "naked vulture." This refers to the condor's bald head. *Californianus* refers to the condor's range.

California is home to 128 wild condors.

Condors usually feed on the remains of large animals.

Masters of the Skies

California condors are the largest land birds in North America. Adults are 3 to 3.5 feet (1–1.1 m) long. Their wingspans extend 9.5 feet (3 m) across. That is approximately the height of a house's ceiling. Condors' wide wingspans help them soar through the air for hours. The birds fly at up to 55 miles per hour (89 km/h).

These masters of the skies soar to find food. They eat carrion, the remains of dead animals. Condors prefer large animals, such as deer, cattle, or sheep. Birds living along the coast might eat sea lions and whales. Some vultures use their sense of smell to find food. Condors use sight instead. When a condor lands to eat, other condors soon join it. Condors are social birds. They often roost near one another. They communicate with grunts, hisses, and wheezes.

Clean Eaters

A condor's bald head is an adaptation to the type of food it eats. It keeps the condor clean. Without feathers, rotting food cannot stick to the bird's face and neck. Condors like to stay clean and neat. They rub against rocks and grass to clean their heads and necks. They wash, smooth, and dry their feathers. These clean habits keep condors healthy.

Life as a California Condor

California condors form long-term pair bonds. They do not build nests. Instead they find a sheltered cliff edge or a cave. They lay their eggs right on the

Parents take turns keeping their chick warm.

sandy surface. Females lay one egg every one to two years. The egg is a whitish to pale green-blue color. Adults incubate their eggs for 54 to 58 days. After that, the chick hatches. It can take days for a condor chick to break out of its egg.

A newly hatched chick is helpless. Fluffy, white down covers its body. But its head, neck, and belly are bare. It depends on its parents for warmth and food. After eight weeks, the chick ventures outside the nest site. But it does not start flying until it is six to seven months old. A young condor stays with its parents for up to two years. It does not fully mature until it is five or six years old.

Ancient Scavengers

California condors lived in much of North America during the Pleistocene epoch, which lasted from 2.6 million to 11,700 years ago. Condors may have scavenged the remains of mammoths and other giant mammals. But the giant mammals gradually died off. So did the condors.

In 1805 the Lewis and Clark expedition spotted a condor in the Pacific Northwest. By that time, the birds lived only along the Pacific coast.

California Condors in Florida?

There is fossil evidence of condors as far east as Florida. The birds' range extended this far during the Pleistocene epoch. Many plants and animals living today got their start during this period. Giant mammals and birds also roamed the continent during this time. Condors likely scavenged the carcasses of species such as the saber-toothed cat.

15

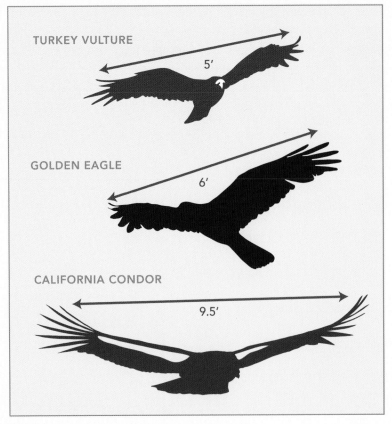

The Largest North American Birds
This chart compares the size of North America's largest birds. How might the condor's size help it survive? How might its size make it harder to survive?

They soared the skies from Baja California, Mexico, to British Columbia, Canada.

Scavenging for Survival

During the 1800s, human development drastically decreased the condor population. Today the condor's range is just a few small pockets in the Southwest. This includes the Grand Canyon and mountainous regions in Arizona and California. Condors also live in the mountains of Baja California. Adult condors have few natural predators in the scrub and forests of the mountains. Chicks are vulnerable to ravens and golden eagles. But the most dangerous condor predator was and still is humans.

EXPLORE ONLINE

Chapter Two discusses California condor characteristics, behavior, and habitat. The website below has more information on the California condor. As you know, every source is different. How is the information on this website similar to what you read in the this chapter? What new facts did you discover?

Birds: California Condor
mycorelibrary.com/california-condor

CHAPTER THREE

THREATS TO CONDORS

Since the 1800s, California condors have faced many threats from humans. Humans have moved onto condor habitat. This brings new dangers closer to condors. Food becomes harder to find. People used to hunt condors. But the most dangerous threat to condors is lead poisoning from ammunition.

As Americans moved west, towns and cities took over land condors used to find food.

Human Threats

Americans moved west in the mid-1800s. Their actions damaged the condor population. They shot and poisoned condors. They took condor eggs.

This had a serious effect on the species. Condors are slow to reproduce. It can take years for them to recover from population losses. In the mid-1910s, the government made it illegal to kill condors.

Harm from Human Development

California condors used to live along the entire US Pacific coast. But today their range is limited to a small, mountainous region in the Southwest. Americans have built homes and towns in condor habitats. City blocks replaced the open range where condors looked for food. The birds migrated farther into the mountains, away from humans. The condors' numbers dwindled. In 1967 they were placed on the federal Endangered Species List. This list keeps track of the United States' most vulnerable species.

Power lines killed this condor in 1966.

Wind Turbine Trouble

Wind is a promising source of renewable energy. But it could have drawbacks for condors. Hundreds of thousands of birds die every year from collisions with wind turbine blades. Wind farm developers are finding ways to avoid these collisions. Some condors have GPS tags so scientists can track them. One California wind farm uses a system to sense condor tags. If the system spots a condor, it shuts the farm down. The process takes just two minutes.

Modern structures continue to threaten condors. Power lines crisscross the skies. Soaring condors fly into the lines. The birds are electrocuted and killed. Wind farms may also pose a threat. Wind turbines can tower more than 328 feet (100 m) high. Their blades can be 116 feet (35 m) long. If a condor collides with them, the bird could die.

Human trash also threatens condors. Microtrash is especially dangerous. This includes small pieces of trash, such as can tabs and bits of plastic. Birds cannot digest these bits of trash. Adult condors

Small bits of trash can kill chicks.

can pass them. But small chicks cannot. Adult birds unwittingly bring microtrash back to the nest for their young. These small bits get stuck in chicks' digestive systems. This blocks other food from being digested. These chicks often starve to death.

Lead Poisoning

Human development and hunting helped send California condor numbers into decline. But the

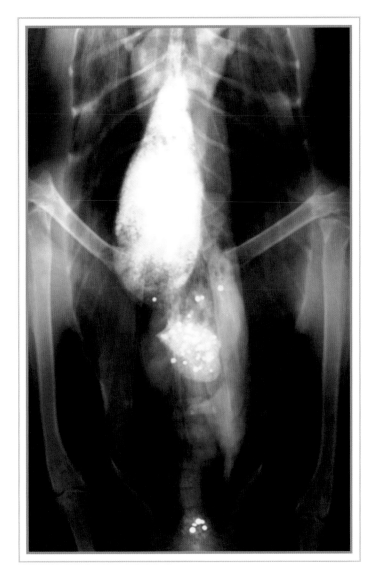

Lead bullet fragments in birds can be seen in X-ray images.

largest and most persistent threat is lead poisoning.
Lead poisoning in birds was first recognized in 1842
in Germany. Americans first noticed it in waterfowl in
the late 1800s. Lead is a soft metal. It is toxic to both

humans and condors. A tiny piece can cause serious health effects. When a condor ingests lead, it loses weight. It loses red blood cells in a condition called anemia. Its wings droop so it cannot fly. Eventually, lead poisoning will result in death.

Condors are exposed to lead through lead ammunition. Scientists know this because they find pieces of lead ammunition in the birds' digestive systems. The type of lead found in condor blood samples matches that used in lead ammunition. Hunters and ranchers use lead ammunition to kill other animals. It breaks apart when it hits its target. It spreads through the dead animal's body. Then condors scavenge meat

Alternative Ammunition

Many hunters are interested in preserving wild animals. One of the best ways to help condors is to switch to nonlead ammunition. Nonlead ammunition is made of copper or copper alloys. These bullets do not break up once they hit their targets. Pieces are not left behind.

from these animals. The birds ingest pieces of the lead ammunition.

Biologists monitor condors that have been released into the wild. They test wild condors for lead. Between 45 and 95 percent test positive in any given year. Experts believe every young bird in the wild today will need treatment for lead poisoning before reaching adulthood. Approximately half of wild condors die of lead poisoning.

Condors still struggle against all these threats. Human activity can hurt the condor. But humans are also working to save the species. With their efforts, condor numbers are growing.

A 2013 California law requires hunters to use nonlead ammunition. The first phase of the law took effect in July 2015. It banned lead ammunition on California Department of Fish and Wildlife lands. In July 2016, the law extended to game birds and small mammals across the state:

> Starting July 1, 2016, nonlead shot will be required when taking upland game birds with a shotgun in California. . . . In addition, nonlead shot will be required when using a shotgun to take resident small game mammals, furbearing mammals, nongame mammals, nongame birds and any wildlife for depredation purposes. . . . The next phase of the implementation goes into effect July 1, 2019, when hunters must use nonlead ammunition when taking any animal anywhere in the state for any purpose. There are no restrictions on the use of lead ammunition for target shooting purposes.

Source: "Nonlead Ammunition Implementation Phase 2 Starts July 1." California Department of Fish and Wildlife News. *California Department of Fish and Wildlife*, *June 28, 2016. Web. Accessed July 1, 2016.*

Changing Minds

This text discusses the steps toward eliminating lead ammunition in California. Imagine you are writing to a California lawmaker. Explain how these changes will help condors. Use facts and details from this book to support your argument.

Hopper Mountain

NATIONAL WILDLIFE REFUGE

U.S. Fish and Wildlife Service
Department of the Interior

Condor Recovery Program

CONDOR CONSERVATION

Scientists, conservation groups, and governments have worked for nearly a century to save California condors. Starting in 1939, the National Audubon Society (NAS) funded the work of biologist Carl Koford. Koford wrote a life history of the California condor species. In the 1930s and 1940s, the NAS pressured the government. The group wanted the government to set aside land

Today the Hopper Mountain National Wildlife Refuge borders the Sespe Condor Sanctuary.

for the condor. The US Forest Service created two condor sanctuaries. In 1947 it set aside land for the Sespe Condor Sanctuary in California. It was one of the early efforts to save condors. It kept condor habitat safe from human disturbance. Today it is 53,000 acres (21,400 ha). The Forest Service also established the Sisquoc Condor Sanctuary in Santa Barbara County, California.

There was also an early attempt to breed condors in captivity. It started in 1952 at the San Diego Zoo. But it was not successful. The science of captive breeding was very new. Koford and other scientists thought the efforts put condors in danger. They worried the program would split up condor pairs. They convinced the government to stop the captive breeding program.

Not Giving Up

In 1966 the US Fish and Wildlife Service (USFWS) stepped in. It appointed biologist Fred Sibley and later Sandy Wilbur to research the condor's decline.

The captive breeding effort in 1952 failed, but conservationists have since raised many condor chicks in captivity.

In 1979 the USFWS created the California Condor Recovery Program (CCRP). It united many private and public organizations in an effort to save condors. In 1980 the USFWS partnered with the NAS. They created the Condor Research Center in Ventura, California. The center took an accurate count of wild condors, monitored wild bird behavior, and documented how and when birds died.

Hatching Hope

The condor population continued to fall. In 1982 there were only 22 wild California condors in the world. People searched months for condor eggs. They took four eggs from the wild in early 1983. The San Diego Zoo received those eggs. It incubated them. It hoped the eggs would hatch. On March 30, 1983, one egg started to crack. The chick inside was hard at work trying to break free. Human handlers helped him. Soon a condor chick's bald head poked out of the egg. Sisquoc had made his way into the world. He was the first condor to hatch in captivity.

Handlers limited human contact with Sisquoc. They used a puppet that looked like an adult condor. This puppet acted as Sisquoc's mother. Using the puppet, handlers fed and interacted with the chick.

Sisquoc became the first male condor in the San Diego Zoo's breeding program. Biologists hoped the program would save the species. Sisquoc went on to

Keepers take a captive condor's egg as it's laid. This can cause the condor to lay another egg. The keepers incubate the first egg.

father 17 chicks in captivity. Twelve of these chicks were released into the wild.

There are many conservation efforts at work today. Some people breed captive condors. They release the offspring into the wild. Other people work to ban lead ammunition. Still others treat lead poisoning. Together, these efforts make up the modern CCRP.

Captive Breeding

Sisquoc was the first condor to hatch at a zoo. But biologists had taken his egg from the wild. To be truly successful, zoologists needed captive condors to breed. By the 1980s, captive breeding techniques had greatly improved. It was time to try breeding condors in captivity once again. The NAS, San Diego Zoo, and USFWS pushed for captive breeding. The San Diego Zoo would breed the birds. So would the Los Angeles Zoo. The Condor Research Center supported the efforts.

Between 1982 and 1987, all the world's condors had either died or been brought into captivity. AC9 had mated with AC8 in 1986. The USFWS caught her in June 1986. It took AC8 and AC9's egg for its condor breeding program. In spring 1987, AC9 was the last wild condor. On April 19, 1987, AC9 was captured. There were no more wild condors. If condors could not breed in captivity, they would go extinct.

The breeding program succeeded on April 29, 1988. Molloko, the first captive-bred condor, hatched. Over the next five years, the condor population

Biologists worked together in the 1980s to capture the remaining wild condors.

more than doubled. It was all thanks to the breeding program. Others joined the effort. Today, the Los Angeles, San Diego, and Oregon zoos still breed condors. So does the Peregrine Fund. They have brought the condor back from near extinction.

Captive breeding is one of the most successful efforts to save the condor. As of December 2015, there were 435 condors in captivity and the wild. All are the descendants of 14 birds, called founders.

Captive Release

Captive breeding made sure the condor would survive. But conservationists wanted more. They wanted the condor to soar freely again. This was and

Older wild birds mentor young, captive-bred birds that are released into the wild.

is the end goal of the CCRP. Conservationists hoped to release condors into the wild.

By 1991 the captive breeding program was working. There were more than 50 condors. The next year, two young condors were released into Southern California. Program participants continued to release captive-bred birds. In 2001 released pairs of condors laid their first eggs. These eggs did not hatch. But it was a start.

Today 10 to 15 chicks hatch in the wild each year. The Santa Barbara Zoo helps monitor their nests.

They check on chicks as they grow. They help chicks if they become ill. Scientists continue to release birds into the wild. The CCRP releases approximately 50 condors each year.

Biologists monitor the condors they release into the wild. They give each bird a number. The practice began in the 1980s with AC9's fellow condors. Birds are tagged with their numbers. This allows for easy identification in the wild. Today some condors wear a GPS tag or radio transmitter. This allows biologists to locate individual birds. They can collect data on where and how the bird spends its time. The San Diego Zoo keeps track of individual birds in a database. This database is

Wing Tags

Bird watchers might notice something odd about wild condors. Each bird has a tag attached to its wing. The tag has a number. These numbers are generally assigned in chronological order. Older birds have smaller numbers. Younger birds have larger ones. The numbers identify each bird.

called a studbook. The studbook records each bird's number. It also lists the bird's hatch date and gender. It even lists the tag numbers of the bird's parents. This data helps track the CCRP's success.

Getting Rid of Lead

According to the USFWS, condors will not recover unless lead poisoning stops. As part of the CCRP, biologists trap condors twice a year. They test the birds' blood for lead poisoning.

In 2013 the state of California passed a law banning lead ammunition. By 2019 only nonlead ammunition can be used. Hunters must switch to nonlead ammunition. So must farmers and ranchers. Arizona and Utah do not regulate the use of lead ammunition. But the Arizona Game and Fish Department encourages hunters to switch to nonlead ammunition. Utah, through a partnership with the Peregrine Fund, offers free nonlead ammunition. This ammunition is available to hunters within the condor's range. The Arizona Game and Fish

Veterinarians regularly test and treat wild condors for lead poisoning.

Department and the Ventana Wildlife Society also offer free nonlead ammunition.

There is evidence the California law and the programs in Arizona and Utah are working. In 2014 just 13 birds required treatment for lead poisoning. The year prior, 28 had required treatment.

Hunters who use nonlead ammunition do more than just prevent lead poisoning. The remains they leave behind are a valuable food source for condors. Safe food will help condors thrive.

In 2015 there were more than 400 California condors. More than 200 lived in the wild. More than 30 years of conservation efforts have saved the species. The CCRP is entering its final phase. The end goal is to have two self-sustaining populations of wild condors. These populations will not need captive breeding programs. With the tireless efforts of biologists and conservationists, that goal could be reached by 2026. When it is, California condors will once again be the masters of the skies.

The Endangered Species Act

The US Congress passed the Endangered Species Act in 1973. The law protects species at risk of becoming extinct. It also protects species that are likely to become endangered. It is illegal to hunt or kill species the law protects. The law also provides funding for conservation programs. One program is the CCRP.

In 2012 the USFWS released a report of the progress of the CCRP in Arizona and Utah:

> *For the first five-year review period (1996-2001): 47 individuals were released; 18 (38%) died or went missing; 2 (4%) birds were returned to captivity . . . for the first fifteen years of the reintroduction program (1996-2011): 134 individuals were released; 61 (46%) died or went missing; 9 (7%) released birds were returned to captivity; 15 wild-hatched chicks were produced; 8 (53%) died or went missing; overall, there were 149 individuals in the population; a total of 69 (46%) died or went missing; and 9 (6%) were returned to captivity*

> Source: Southwest Condor Review Team. "A Review of the Third Five Years of the California Condor Reintroduction Program in the Southwest (2007–2011)." Pacific Southwest Office. US Fish and Wildlife Service, May 2012. PDF file.

What's the Big Idea?

Read the report on this page carefully. What is the main idea of the passage? What conclusions can you draw from the two sets of statistics? Use details from the passage to support your answers.

SPECIES OVERVIEW

Common Name

- California condor

Scientific Name

- *Gymnogyps californianus*

Average Size

- 3 to 3.5 feet (0.9–1.1 m) long from beak to tail
- 17 to 25 pounds (7–11 kg)
- Approximately 9.5 foot (3 m) wingspan

Color

- Black feathers, white patches under wings, and an orange to reddish-purple head

Diet

- Carrion, including deer, cattle, and sheep

Average Life Span

- Estimated at up to 60 years

Habitat

- Mountainous regions in California and Arizona, such as the Grand Canyon, and Baja California, Mexico

Threats

- Human development, historical hunting, and lead poisoning
- Endangered status: critically endangered

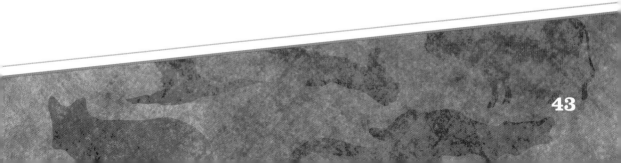

STOP AND THINK

Tell the Tale

Chapter Four discusses how biologists at the San Diego Zoo bred and raised Sisquoc. Imagine you are a biologist taking care of young Sisquoc. Write a journal entry that describes a typical day for you and Sisquoc.

Say What?

Studying conservation efforts to save California condors can mean learning a lot of new vocabulary. Find five words in this book that you've never heard before. Use a dictionary or the Internet to find out what they mean. Write down the meanings of each word. Then use each word in a new sentence.

Dig Deeper

After reading this book, what questions do you still have about California condors? With an adult's help, find a few reliable sources that can help you answer your questions. Write a paragraph about what you learned.

Surprise Me

Chapter Three describes threats to the California condor. After reading this book, what condor threat surprised you the most? Write a few sentences describing the threat and why you found it surprising.

GLOSSARY

adaptation
a change in an animal that helps it survive in its environment

alloys
substances made of metals and other materials melted together

carrion
dead and decaying animal meat

conservation
preserving and protecting something

digest
to break down food into nutrients the body can use

fletch
to arrange feathers on an arrow

GPS
the global positioning system, which uses satellites to find the location of objects

mature
fully grown up

predators
animals that hunt and eat other animals

range
an area where an animal lives

species
a group of animals or plants that share basic traits

LEARN MORE

Books

Alderfer, Jonathan. *National Geographic Kids Bird Guide of North America: The Best Birding Book for Kids from National Geographic's Bird Experts.* Washington, DC: National Geographic, 2013.

Gray, Susan H. *California Condor.* Ann Arbor, MI: Cherry Lake Publishing, 2013.

Hoare, Ben, and Tom Jackson. *Endangered Animals.* New York: DK Publishing, 2010.

Websites

To learn more about Back from Near Extinction, visit **booklinks.abdopublishing.com**. These links are routinely monitored and updated to provide the most current information available.

Visit **mycorelibrary.com** for free additional tools for teachers and students.

INDEX

ABOUT THE AUTHOR

Amanda Lanser is a freelance writer who lives in Minnesota. She and her husband are animal lovers. Amanda enjoys birding in her free time. She hopes to see a wild California condor one day.